Words of Love

Words of Love

A Tapestry of Love
from the World's Greatest Poetry

Norcross

Grateful acknowledgment is made to the following for permission to reprint previously published material:
The Belknap Press of Harvard University Press, Cambridge, Massachusetts, and the Trustees of Amherst College: "We Learned the Whole of Love," "Love—thou art high—" (last twelve lines) from *The Poems of Emily Dickinson,* Edited by Thomas H. Johnson. Copyright © 1951, 1955, by The President and Fellows of Harvard College. Harcourt Brace Jovanovich, Inc.: "Love is a Deep and a Dark and a Lonely," "Foxgloves," "If So Hap May Be," "Sundancer," excerpt from "Impasse" from *Honey and Salt* by Carl Sandburg. Copyright © 1963 by Carl Sandburg. Harper & Row, Publishers, Inc.: and Norma Millay Ellis for "When I too long have looked upon your face," "I do but ask that you always be fair," "Being Young and Green," "Song for Young Lovers in a City" from *Collected Poems of Edna St. Vincent Millay.* Copyright 1921, 1922, 1948, 1950 by Edna St. Vincent Millay. Little, Brown and Company: "Love—thou art high—" (first six lines) from *The Complete Poems of Emily Dickinson,* Edited by Thomas H. Johnson. Copyright © 1929, 1957 by Mary L. Hampson.

Creative Director: Eleanor Ehrhardt

Associate: Sue Tarsky

Design Assistant: Charlotte Staub

Photographs:

Kevin Lammens; Charles R. Luchsinger.

ontents

Carl Sandburg

was born in 1878, the son of Swedish immigrant parents. He lived in the small town of Galesburg, Illinois. When he was twenty-five years old he moved to Chicago, where he worked as a newspaper reporter and editor. In 1908 he married Lilian Paula Steichen.

Sandburg was practically unknown until the publication of his *Chicago Poems* in 1916. The vivid style and language of his poetry brought him into the public eye.

Sandburg's poetry abounds in love—love for the common man, love for his country, love for the earth itself. Sandburg held many different jobs during his early years; he even rode freight trains with hobos. His varied experiences kept him close to the people and gave him both a familiarity with their language and a feeling for the simple things in life. Sandburg believed in people, and this belief, together with his natural optimism and idealism, is reflected with clarity in all of his poems.

In 1940 Sandburg was awarded the Pulitzer Prize for history, and in 1950, the Pulitzer Prize for poetry. He received numerous other awards and citations until his death in Flat Rock, North Carolina, in 1967.

Tell us again: Nothing is impossible.
We listen while you tell us.

Carl Sandburg

Foxgloves

Your heart was handed over
to the foxgloves one hot summer afternoon.
The snowsilk buds nodded and hung drowsy.
   So the stalks believed
   As they held those buds above.
   In deep wells of white
The dark fox fingers go in these gloves.
   In a slow fold of summer
Your heart was handed over in a curve
   from bud to bloom.

Carl Sandburg

Love is a Deep and a Dark and a Lonely

love is a deep and a dark and a lonely
and you take it deep take it dark
and take it with a lonely winding
and when the winding gets too lonely
then may come the windflowers
and the breath of wind over many flowers
winding its way out of many lonely flowers
waiting in rainleaf whispers
waiting in dry stalks of noon
wanting in a music of windbreaths
so you can take love as it comes keening
as it comes with a voice and a face
and you make a talk of it
talking to yourself a talk worth keeping
and you put it away for a keen keeping
and you find it to be a hoarding
and you give it away and yet it stays hoarded

like a book read over and over again
like one book being a long row of books
like leaves of windflowers bending low
and bending to be never broken

Carl Sandburg

If So Hap May Be

Be somber with those in smoke garments.
Laugh with those eating bitter weeds.
Burn your love with bold flame blossoms,
    if so hap may be.
Leave him with a soft snowfall memory,
    if so hap may be

       • •

    Never came winter stars more clear
    yet the stars lost themselves
    midnight came snow-wrought snow-blown.

Carl Sandburg

Sun Dancer

Spider, you have long silver legs.
You may spin diagrams of doom.
Your patterns may throw fine glints
Festooned from wandering silk.
It may be neither art nor money
Nor calisthenics nor engineering.
No man trusts any woman and vice versa.
All men love all women and vice versa.
And all friends cherish each other.
And there are triflers who flirt with death.
Spider, you have long silver legs.

Carl Sandburg

illiam Blake

was born in 1757 in London, England. As a youth he began to write poetry and displayed a powerful artistic imagination. Many of his works were inspired by visions, which he claimed to have had from childhood.

Blake earned his living as an engraver and book illustrator, accepting commissions from publishers and private patrons. Among his most famous works were illustrations of the Bible. By 1788 he had devised an original technique for engraving text and pictures on the same plate; the resulting prints were then colored by hand. Nearly all of his own poems and drawings were printed in this manner.

Absorbed in his work, Blake passed a quiet life in London with his wife, Catherine, who assisted him with his printmaking.

If any could desire what he is incapable of possessing, despair must be his eternal lot.

William Blake

Song

Love and harmony combine,
And around our souls intwine,
While thy branches mix with mine,
And our roots together join.

Joys upon our branches sit,
Chirping loud, and singing sweet;
Like gentle streams beneath our feet
Innocence and virtue meet.

William Blake

To the Evening Star

Thou fair-hair'd angel of the evening,
Now, whilst the sun rests on the mountains, light
Thy bright torch of love; thy radiant crown
Put on, and smile upon our evening bed!
Smile on our loves, and, while thou drawest the
Blue curtains of the sky, scatter thy silver dew
On every flower that shuts its sweet eyes
In timely sleep. Let thy west wind sleep on
The lake; speak silence with thy glimmering eyes,
And wash the dusk with silver. Soon, full soon,
Dost thou withdraw; then the wolf rages wide,
And the lion glares thro' the dun forest:
The fleeces of our flocks are cover'd with
Thy sacred dew: protect them with thine influence.

William Blake

Percy Bysshe Shelly

was born in 1792 to a wealthy family in Sussex, England. He studied at Oxford University, but was expelled for co-authoring a pamphlet on atheism. At the age of nineteen he met young Harriet Westbrook. She fell in love with him and, against her parents' wishes, they eloped. The marriage was not a happy one; in 1814 Shelley became involved with Mary Godwin (who later wrote the famous horror story *Frankenstein*). The lovers left England together and when Shelley's wife committed suicide a few years later, Shelley and Mary Godwin married. They lived in Switzerland, where they became close friends of Lord Byron, and later settled in Italy. There Shelley drowned in a sailing mishap at the age of thirty.

Shelley was a Romantic, writing poetry to help fight against the oppressors of the world, both socially and intellectually. He had faith in mankind, but his trust was founded in the intellect. Because of this belief, Shelley looked at the past golden age of Greece as his model for the future of the world.

How shall ever one like me
Win thee back again?

Percy Bysshe Shelley

Her voice is hovering o'er my soul—it lingers
  O'ershadowing it with soft and lulling wings,
The blood and life within those snowy fingers
  Teach witchcraft to the instrumental strings.
My brain is wild, my breath comes quick—
  The blood is listening in my frame,
And thronging shadows, fast and thick,
  Fall on my overflowing eyes;
My heart is quivering like a flame;
  As morning dew, that in the sunbeam dies,
I am dissolved in these consuming ecstasies.

Percy Bysshe Shelley

Lord Byron

was born George Gordon Byron in 1788 in London, England. When he was three years old his father died, leaving very little money, and his mother took him to live in Scotland. He returned to England at the age of ten and inherited the title Lord Byron. By the time he was twenty-three he was already an established poet, having become famous almost overnight with the publication of *Childe Harold's Pilgrimage.*

Although born lame, Byron was a handsome man and popular with women. He was married in 1815 to Anne Isabella Milbanke. When she took their baby daughter and left him in 1816, Byron fled England. He went to Italy, where he fell in love with the Countess Teresa Guiccioli. In 1822 he went to fight for the Greeks in their struggle for independence from Turkey. He died of a fever in Greece at the age of thirty-six.

Byron searched for the ideal in everything, and so was always disappointed by the reality. His poetry reflects this constant search and disappointment.

She Walks in Beauty

She walks in Beauty, like the night
    Of cloudless climes and starry skies;
And all that's best of dark and bright
    Meet in her aspect and her eyes:
Thus mellowed to that tender light
    Which Heaven to gaudy day denies.

One shade the more, one ray the less,
    Had half impaired the nameless grace
Which waves in every raven tress,
    Or softly lightens o'er her face;
Where thoughts serenely sweet express,
    How pure, how dear their dwelling-place.

And on that cheek, and o'er that brow,
    So soft, so calm, yet eloquent,
The smiles that win, the tints that glow,
    But tell of days in goodness spent,
A mind at peace with all below,
    A heart whose love is innocent!

Lord Byron

We'll Go No More a-Roving

So we'll go no more a-roving
    So late into the night,
Though the heart be still as loving,
    And the moon be still as bright.

For the sword outwears its sheath,
    And the soul wears out the breast,
And the heart must pause to breathe,
    And Love itself have rest.

Though the night was made for loving,
    And the day returns too soon,
Yet we'll go no more a-roving
    By the light of the moon.

Lord Byron

ohn Keats

was born in 1795 in London, England, into a middle-class family. When he was only eight years old his father died; when he was fifteen he lost his mother. Forced to leave school, he became apprenticed to a surgeon. Poetry proved to be a greater lure, however, and he gave up his medical career to devote himself to writing.

Deeply in love with Fanny Brawne, Keats tried valiantly to publish a book that could earn enough money to enable them to marry. In just one year he produced a remarkable number of poems, but to no avail; his work was not appreciated by the critics.

Keats was already ill with tuberculosis, and now the disease worsened. Hoping to find relief in a warmer climate, he left by himself for Italy. He and Fanny were never reunited and Keats died in Rome at the age of twenty-five.

When I Have Fears

When I have fears that I may cease to be
   Before my pen has glean'd my teeming brain,
Before high-piled books, in charact'ry,
   Hold like rich garners the full-ripen'd grain;
When I behold, upon the night's starr'd face,
   Huge cloudy symbols of a high romance,
And think that I may never live to trace
   Their shadows, with the magic hand of chance;
And when I feel, fair creature of an hour,
   That I shall never look upon thee more,
Never have relish in the faery power
   Of unreflecting love!—then on the shore
Of the wide world I stand alone, and think
Till Love and Fame to nothingness do sink.

John Keats

illiam Shakespeare

was born in 1564 in the English country town of Stratford-on-Avon. He was one of eight children. At that time, his father was a prosperous glove-maker and town official.

William finished grammar school, but could not afford to go on to the university because by then his father had suffered serious business reverses. At eighteen he married Anne Hathaway, who was eight years his senior. Their first daughter, Susanna, was born shortly thereafter and twins, Hamnet and Judith, arrived three years later.

Shakespeare moved to London, leaving his family in Stratford, and soon joined a theatrical repertory company. He was first an actor, then a playwright. His works were immediate commercial successes. After twenty years in London he moved back to Stratford, where he spent his final days as a country gentleman.

At his death in 1616 Shakespeare left an unequaled legacy—34 plays, 154 sonnets, and two major long poems.

As an unperfect actor on the stage,
Who with his fear is put besides his part,
Or some fierce thing replete with too much rage,
Whose strength's abundance weakens his own heart,
So I, for fear of trust, forget to say
The perfect ceremony of love's rite,
And in mine own love's strength seem to decay,
O'ercharged with burden of mine own love's might.
Oh, let my books be then the eloquence
And dumb presagers of my speaking breast,
Who plead for love, and look for recompense,
More than that tongue that more hath more expressed.
   Oh, learn to read what silent love hath writ.
   To hear with eyes belongs to love's fine wit.

William Shakespeare

Let me not to the marriage of true minds
Admit impediments. Love is not love
Which alters when it alteration finds,
Or bends with the remover to remove.
Oh, no! it is an ever-fixèd mark
That looks on tempests and is never shaken;
It is the star to every wandering bark,
Whose worth's unknown, although his height be
   taken.
Love's not Time's fool, though rosy lips and cheeks
Within his bending sickle's compass come;
Love alters not with his brief hours and weeks,
But bears it out even to the edge of doom.
   If this be error and upon me proved,
   I never writ, nor no man ever loved.

William Shakespeare

When, in disgrace with fortune and men's eyes,
I all alone beweep my outcast state
And trouble deaf heaven with my bootless cries
And look upon myself and curse my fate,
Wishing me like to one more rich in hope,
Featured like him, like him with friends possessed,
Desiring this man's art and that man's scope,
With what I most enjoy contented least;
Yet in these thoughts myself almost despising,
Haply I think on thee, and then my state,
Like to the lark at break of day arising
From sullen earth, sings hymns at heaven's gate;
    For thy sweet love remembered such wealth
       brings
    That then I scorn to change my state with kings.

William Shakespeare

lfred Lord Tennyson

was born in 1809 in Somersby, Lincoln-shire, England.

As a young man Tennyson was filled with great anxiety, depression, and doubt, which are reflected in many of his poems.

From 1816 to 1820 he attended the Grammar School at Louth. He was unhappy there and received permission to return home where his father became his tutor until he entered Trinity College, Cambridge, in 1828.

He formed a close relationship at Cambridge with Arthur Henry Hallam, son of the historian, who helped draw Tennyson out of his deep reserve. It was a great blow to Tennyson when Hallam died in 1833. He grieved for years and in 1850 arranged the elegies he had composed into his famous poem *In Memoriam.*

When Tennyson was forty-one he married Emily Sellwood, and the second half of his life was happy, secure, and filled with poetic accomplishments. In 1884 he was given the title Baron Tennyson of Freshwater and Aldworth.

He died in 1892 and was buried in Westminster Abbey.

*'Tis better to have loved and lost
Than never to have loved at all.*

Alfred Lord Tennyson

In Memoriam

I cannot love thee as I ought,
   For love reflects the thing beloved;
   My words are only words, and moved
Upon the topmost froth of thought.

"Yet blame not thou thy plaintive song,"
   The Spirit of true love replied;
   "Thou canst not move me from thy side,
Nor human frailty do me wrong.

"What keeps a spirit wholly true
   To that ideal which he bears?
   What record? not the sinless years
That breathed beneath the Syrian blue;

"So fret not, like an idle girl,
   That life is dash'd with flecks of sin.
   Abide; thy wealth is gather'd in,
When Time hath sunder'd shell from pearl."

Alfred Lord Tennyson

dna St. Vincent Millay

was born in Maine on February 22, 1892. Her parents were divorced in 1900 and although struggling with poverty, her mother encouraged her to excel in music and poetry.

Her first poems were published by a magazine when she was 14 years old.

With the financial assistance of friends, she entered Vassar College in 1913. While there she acted in Vassar productions of several plays, including one which she had written. She graduated in 1917, the year her first volume, *Renascence and Other Poems,* was published.

Her love of acting took her to New York to join the Provincetown Players, during which time she lived in Greenwich Village.

In 1920 she left for Europe to write for *Vanity Fair.* She continued to write poetry and in 1922 her novel, *Hardigut,* was published. In 1923 she returned to the United States and married Eugen Jan Boissevain. They bought a farm at Austerlitz, New York, their home for the rest of their lives.

She was deeply committed to the equal rights for women movement, and on November 17, 1923, called on the President with a group from the National Women's Party. She continued to be an advocate of justice and was a modern humanist in her writings until her death in 1950.

Song for Young Lovers in a City

Though less for love than for the deep
Though transient death that follows it
These childish mouths grown soft in sleep
Here in a rented bed have met,

They have not met in love's despite . . .
Such tiny loves will leap and flare
Lurid as coke-fires in the night,
Against a background of despair.

To treeless grove, to grey retreat
Descend in flocks from corniced eaves
The pigeons now on sooty·feet,
To cover them with linden leaves.

Edna St. Vincent Millay

I do but ask that you be always fair,
That I for ever may continue kind;
Knowing me what I am, you should not dare
To lapse from beauty ever, nor seek to bind
My alterable mood with lesser cords:
Weeping and such soft matters but invite
To further vagrancy, and bitter words
Chafe soon to irremediable flight.
Wherefore I pray you if you love me dearly
Less dear to hold me than your own bright charms
Whence it may fall that until death or nearly
I shall not move to struggle from your arms;
Fade if you must; I would but bid you be
Like the sweet year, doing all things graciously.

Edna St. Vincent Millay

When I too long have looked upon your face,
Wherein for me a brightness unobscured
Save by the mists of brightness has its place,
And terrible beauty not to be endured,
I turn away reluctant from your light,
And stand irresolute, a mind undone,
A silly, dazzled thing deprived of sight
From having looked too long upon the sun.
Then is my daily life a narrow room
In which a little while, uncertainly,
Surrounded by impenetrable gloom,
Among familiar things grown strange to me
Making my way, I pause, and feel, and hark,
Till I become accustomed to the dark.

Edna St. Vincent Millay

Being Young and Green

Being young and green, I said in love's despite:
Never in the world will I to living wight
Give over, air my mind
To anyone,
Hang out its ancient secrets in the strong wind
To be shredded and faded. . . .

Oh, me, invaded
And sacked by the wind and the sun!

Edna St. Vincent Millay

Elizabeth Barrett Browning

was born to a wealthy family in 1806 in Herefordshire, England, the eldest of eleven children. At fifteen she suffered a spinal injury which left her in fragile health. Shortly afterward her family moved to London, where she developed tuberculosis. In a well-meaning attempt to protect his daughter, Elizabeth's father confined her to her room.

As a semi-invalid she found pleasure in studying and writing, and she soon established a reputation as a fine poet. Robert Browning admired her work and began writing to her. When they met, he proposed marriage. Elizabeth's father, still fearful for her health, strongly opposed the union. The couple married secretly in 1846 and fled to Italy where they lived until her death in 1861.

Elizabeth Barrett Browning's most famous work is a series of sonnets inspired by her love for Robert. Because of her dark complexion, Robert had called her his "Little Portuguese," and it was he who gave the sonnets the title *Sonnets from the Portuguese* so that they might be published under the guise of being translations.

I love thee freely . . .
I love thee purely . . .
            —I love thee with the breath,
Smiles, tears, of all my life!—and, if God choose,
I shall but love thee better after death.

Elizabeth Barrett Browning

If thou must love me, let it be for nought
Except for love's sake only. Do not say
"I love her for her smile—her look—her way
Of speaking gently,—for a trick of thought
That falls in well with mine, and certes brought
A sense of pleasant ease on such a day;"—
For these things in themselves, beloved, may
Be changed, or change for thee,—and love so wrought,
May be unwrought so. Neither love me for
Thine own dear pity's wiping my cheeks dry:
A creature might forget to weep, who bore
Thy comfort long, and lose thy love thereby.
But love me for love's sake, that evermore
Thou may'st love on through love's eternity.

Elizabeth Barrett Browning

My letters all dead paper, mute and white!
And yet they seem alive and quivering
Against my tremulous hands which loose the string
And let them drop down on my knee to-night.
This said, he wished to have me in his sight
Once, as a friend; this fixed a day in spring
To come and touch my hand—a simple thing,
Yet I wept for it!—this—the paper's light—
Said, *"Dear,* I love thee"; and I sank and quailed
As if God's future thundered on my past:
This said, "I am thine"—and so its ink has paled
With lying at my heart that beat too fast:
And this—O Love, thy words have ill availed,
If, what this said, I dared repeat at last!

Elizabeth Barrett Browning

obert Browning

was born in 1812 in Camberwell, England. His father owned an extensive library, and from it Robert acquired a knowledge of the arts, the classics, history, and philosophy. His mother instilled in him a deep love of music.

In 1846 Browning married the poet Elizabeth Barrett. Their romance was one of the world's most famous. They lived happily in Florence, Italy, until Elizabeth's death in 1861. Heartbroken, Browning returned to London with their son. The memory of Elizabeth haunted him for the rest of his life, but he found solace in his writing. His beautiful poem *Prospice* shows the depth of his love and his loss. By the time he was sixty he had been acclaimed a great poet. Browning continued to write until the time of his death in 1889.

My soul
Smoothed itself out, a long-cramped scroll
Freshening and fluttering in the wind.

Robert Browning

Meeting at Night

I

The gray sea and the long black land;
And the yellow half-moon large and low;
And the startled little waves that leap
In fiery ringlets from their sleep,
As I gain the cove with pushing prow,
And quench its speed i' the slushy sand.

II

Then a mile of warm sea-scented beach;
Three fields to cross till a farm appears;
A tap at the pane, the quick sharp scratch
And blue spurt of a lighted match,
And a voice less loud, thro' its joys and fears,
Than the two hearts beating each to each!

Robert Browning

Never the Time and the Place

Never the time and the place
  And the loved one all together!
This path—how soft to pace!
  This May—what magic weather!
Where is the loved one's face?
In a dream that loved one's face meets mine,
  But the house is narrow, the place is bleak
Where, outside, rain and wind combine
  With a furtive ear, if I strive to speak,
  With a hostile eye at my flushing cheek,
With a malice that marks each word, each sign
O enemy sly and serpentine,
  Uncoil thee from the waking man!
    Do I hold the Past
    Thus firm and fast
  Yet doubt if the Future hold I can?
This path so soft to pace shall lead
Thro' the magic of May to herself indeed!
Or narrow if needs the house must be.
Outside are the storms and strangers: we—
Oh, close, safe, warm sleep I and she,
  —I and she!

Robert Browning

Love in a Life

Room after room,
I hunt the house through
We inhabit together.
Heart, fear nothing, for, heart, thou shalt find her—
Next time, herself!—not the trouble behind her
Left in the curtain, the couch's perfume!
As she brushed it, the cornice-wreath blossomed anew:
Yon looking-glass gleamed at the wave of her feather.

Yet the day wears,
And door succeeds door;
I try the fresh fortune—
Range the wide house from the wing to the centre.
Still the same chance! she goes out as I enter.
Spend my whole day in the quest,—who cares?
But 'tis twilight, you see,—with such suites to explore,
Such closets to search, such alcoves to importune!

Robert Browning

Prospice

Fear death?—to feel the fog in my throat,
    The mist in my face,
When the snows begin, and the blasts denote
    I am nearing the place,
The power of the night, the press of the storm,
    The post of the foe;
Where he stands, the Arch Fear in a visible form,
    Yet the strong man must go;
For the journey is done and the summit attained,
    And the barriers fall,
Though a battle's to fight ere the guerdon be gained,
    The reward of it all.
I was ever a fighter, so—one fight more,
    The best and the last!
I would hate that death bandaged my eyes, and forbore,
    And bade me creep past.
No! let me taste the whole of it, fare like my peers,
    The heroes of old,
Bear the brunt, in a minute pay glad life's arrears
    Of pain, darkness, and cold.
For sudden the worst turns the best to the brave,
    The black minute's at end,
And the elements' rage, the fiend-voices that rave,
    Shall dwindle, shall blend,
Shall change, shall become first a peace out of pain,
    Then a light, then thy breast,
O thou soul of my soul! I shall clasp thee again,
    And with God be the rest!

Robert Browning

mily Dickinson

was born in 1830 in Amherst, Massachu-
setts, where her grandfather had been one
of the founders of the town, the church, and the college.
Her father was a lawyer, her mother a New England
housewife who "did not care for thought."

In 1847 Emily studied at South Hadley Seminary
and at Amherst Academy.

The winter of 1853 she spent in Washington
where her father was serving in Congress, and during a
visit to Philadelphia she experienced an unhappy love
affair. She firmly renounced the man because she would
not "wreck another woman's life." She subsequently with-
drew into seclusion, seeing no one except a very few in-
tellectual friends and her brother's family who considered
her the "ecstatic daredevil, shy paradox."

Although considered a great poet, she would per-
mit publication of only three or four poems during her
secluded life. Since her death in 1886 several collections
of her beautiful and mystical poetry have appeared.

Love—thou art high—
I cannot climb thee—
But, were it Two—
Who knows but we—
Taking turns—at the Chimborazo—
Ducal—at last—stand up by thee—

Love—thou art deep—
I cannot cross thee—
But, were there Two
Instead of One—
Rower, and Yacht—some sovereign Summer—
Who knows—but we'd reach the Sun?

Love—thou art Veiled—
A few—behold thee—
Smile—and alter—and prattle—and die—
Bliss—were an Oddity—without thee—
Nicknamed by God—
Eternity—

                                    Emily Dickinson

Final Harvest

We learned the Whole of Love—
The Alphabet—the Words—
A Chapter—then the mighty Book—
Then—Revelation closed—

But in Each Other's eyes
An Ignorance beheld—
Diviner than the Childhood's—
And each to each, a Child—

Attempted to expound
What Neither—understood—
Alas, that Wisdom is so large—
And Truth—so manifold!

Emily Dickinson